The Greenleaf Guide to
Famous Men of
Greece

by Cyndy Shearer

Greenleaf Press
Lebanon, Tennessee

www.greenleafpress.com
1570 Old Laguardo Rd
Lebanon, TN 37087
GREENLEAF
P · R · E · S · S

History for the thoughtful child

HOW TO USE THIS GUIDE

Introduction:

When you want to build something, a hammer is a very useful thing to have. But if someone picks up your hammer and starts beating you over the head with it, the hammer is no longer a tool — it's a murder weapon. So it is with text books and study guides. This book is intended to be a tool, a possible model for you to use and adapt as you see fit. You will know what suggestions will work best for the students you teach. I hope you will find it useful.

Putting your study in context:

Before you begin your study of this book, let me suggest that you put it in context — not so much chronological context as biblical. Before our family began to study Famous Men of Greece we went back to the Old Testament and reviewed the first few chapters of Genesis and reread the descriptions of those who followed Adam and sons. We made note of who were the farmers, who were herdsmen, who were workers in what craft. The picture that we saw there was very different from the typical evolutionary picture of homo sapiens gradually leaving his primitive life as "hunter-gatherer" to settle down into more advanced stationary lifestyle. Read through the story of the Tower of Babel. Discuss what you read together with the children you teach.

Once we had covered this material, we turned to the first chapter of Romans and read about what happens when man turns away from the truth and exchanges it for a lie. Again, we saw that the Bible paints a very different picture of the "evolution of religion" than that which is presented by evolutionary doctrines. Evolution teaches that man crawled out of the primordial mush a primitive animist. Our ancestors then gradually evolved to higher, more sophisticated forms of religion — becoming, first, polytheists and then monotheists. (Next step atheists?) The Bible, however, teaches just the opposite — that created man understood that there was one God, but as men turned away, rejecting truth, God turned them over to lies. Man exchanged the truth of monotheism for the lies of polytheism and animism.

How To Use This Guide *(continued)*

When you look at the early history of nations, you often find an initial mix of myth / legend / history. (The weapon used so often against college Christians... "Ah," they often say, "You see, all the cultures of the world have the same myths that the primitive Hebrews had...") So it is important to talk about what the differences and similarities are between myth/legend/history. When you read the creation stories of other nations the differences between them and the biblical record of creation are glaring.

We read the myths and legends of Greece and talked about the characteristics of the gods and goddesses. What could we expect the Greek culture/people to be like, based on what we observed about their religion? Who were their heroes? What were they like? We could do this because we had started with Genesis (and knew how people developed different skills and became different nations) and because we had started with Romans and talked about the devolution of religion. I don't recommend teaching mythology outside of this context.

Methods of Evaluation:

When we think of testing, we usually think of exams — essay questions, true/false, multiple choice. There is a place for traditional testing both in and out of conventional classroom settings, but don't overlook the other options. If after reading a story, or listening to you read it aloud, the child is able to tell you the story in his own words — you can know that he understands it.

Another means by which you can evaluate a student's understanding of a selection is through oral discussion. The "For Discussion" questions provided for each chapter are intended to be suggestions — questions you might ask. Often, as you discuss the reading, you will naturally cover the material without sticking to a rigid "question/answer" format. Treasure those times! Sometimes you will need to draw your students along point by point. Sometimes you will need to ask questions different from those suggested. By all means, do.

Written assignments also help evaluate understanding. Some "For Discussion" questions will work particularly well as essay topics. Occasionally have your students retell the story by presenting it as a news story, short story, play, etc.

Many chapters in the book contain legends or stories told about famous figures and are included because they demonstrate some character trait or attitude valued by or typical of the people of the nation. It is not necessary to approach these chapters in the same way you might approach a chapter about someone like Julius Caesar. There are certain battles, facts, dates and people that make good historical memory work, but all chapters are not created equal in this regard. And remember to go easy on memorizing dates. Its far more important to remember people and important ideas. Dates are easy to look up if we forget.

How To Use This Guide *(continued)*

Summary:

Our goals for the study of history are these:

1. That our students will see that God is involved in all history.
    Because God is involved in all of life, Scripture is relevant to all of life.
    Therefore, all things can and should be evaluated in light of Scripture. As we
    look at how men and women in our history have made choices, we have a unique
    opportunity to evaluate those choices as we see what kinds of endings they
    made for themselves. We can then consider what kind of lives we are building
    for ourselves and modeling for our children. In this way we can use history as a
    means by which God can teach us to number our days and apply our hearts to
    wisdom.

2. That when our students begin to study history in advanced courses they will not
    be starting from scratch, but will be building on a well-laid foundation.
    They will have a general knowledge of important people and events and have a
    good feel for what happened in what order. I do not expect a third grader to
    remember everything I teach about Greece, for instance. But when he studies
    the material again later, he will find himself in familiar territory. Thus he will
    have to memorize less because he will have some familiarity with the people and
    places involved.

    In general, high school level history material is written in a way that assumes
    some prior knowledge of the stories. If you already know the basic facts about,
    say, Pericles when you begin to study him in high school, you have less to
    memorize. You can simply add the additional information to what you already
    know. (One of the things that makes history classes so boring is that very few
    students come to them with such a background. Because everything is new,
    everything must be memorized.)

Textbooks, by themselves, teach you facts. They do not introduce you to real people.
Teaching history to elementary school students should be like calling a child to story
time. You find a snug comfortable place, you curl up together, and you start with "Once
upon a time..."

- Cyndy Shearer

Supplemental Books

The Penguin Historical Atlas of Ancient Greece

The Story of the Iliad, the classic retold by Alfred J. Church
    (Greenleaf Press reprint)

The Children's Homer by Padraic Colum (retelling of the Odyssey)

The Trial and Death of Socrates by Plato

You might also want to utilize some books selected from the following:

Reference:

    Ancient Greece (DK Eyewitness Books)

    Growing Up in Ancient Greece by Chris Chelepi

    The Ancient City: Life in Classical Athens & Rome by Peter Connolly

Literature:

    Classic Myths to Read Aloud by William Russell

    Mythology by Edith Hamilton

    d'Aulaire's Book of Greek Myths

    The Macmillan Book of Greek Gods and Heroes

Activity & Coloring Books:

    Classical Kids: An Activity Guide to Life in Ancient Greece and Rome

    Life in Ancient Greece Coloring Book (Dover History Coloring Book)

The Geography of Greece

1. Study a good relief map of Greece and Crete.
    Locate any mountains, rivers, lakes, deserts.
    What are their names?
    Note: There is 6 level shaded relief map on page 48 – 49 of *The Penguin Atlas of Ancient Greece* and a simple shaded relief map showing major cities and regions on page 6 of the DK Eyewitness *Ancient Greece* book.

MOUNTAINS:	LAKES:
RIVERS:	DESERTS:
OCEANS/SEAS:	OTHER:

The Geography of Greece

(continued)

2. What major cities do you find?

_____

_____

_____

_____

3. Do the geographic features you listed divide the country into separated regions?

_____

_____

What features would provide natural defenses?

_____

_____

What areas of the country are more open to attack?

_____

_____

In what way?

_____

_____

The Geography of Greece

(continued)

4. Where would you expect food to be grown most easily?

   _____

   What other occupations would you expect to find in various regions of the country?

   _____

   _____

5. Take a piece of tracing paper and lay it over the relief map. Using a dark, soft lead pencil, trace the map of Greece. Be sure to include and label major mountains, rivers, lakes, deserts, and cities. Note significant features bordering the areas you are studying.

6. Make a salt map which shows the major features of Greece and Crete.

   Step 1: On an unbendable piece of cardboard (about 15 x 15 inches), draw the outline of Greece and Crete. Be sure and use a pencil.

   Step 2: Make the salt/flour dough
   1 part salt
   2 parts flour
   enough water to make a slightly sticky, but manageable dough
   (1 cup salt, 2 cups flour will make enough dough for two good sized maps.)
   If you would like to color the dough to show differences in elevation or vegetation, add a little food coloring or tempera paint to the dough when you add the water.
   Be sure to use a bowl that won't be stained by the dye.

   Step 3: Take the salt dough and press it into the outline you have drawn on the cardboard. Build up ridges for mountains, make depressions in the dough to show rivers lakes or other low spots. You might want to use tempera paint to paint bordering oceans, nations, etc.

   Step 4: Lay map flat and let it dry overnight.

Introduction

THE GODS OF GREECE

Supplemental Texts:

The Penguin Atlas of Ancient Greece, pages 60-61, "The Classical Myths"

Vocabulary:

myth	exaggerated	invincible
legend	titanic	nymph
trident		

People and Places:

Ti'tan	Hy-per'i-on	At'las
Cro'nus	Pros'er-pine	Dem'e-ter
Zeus	Per-seph'o-ne	Her'a
Cer'ber-us	Cha'ron	Ha'des
Her'mes	He-phaes'tus	A'res
A-pol'lo	Di-an'a	A-the'na
A-phro-di'te	E-ros'	The Graces
The Furies	The Fates	River Styx

For Discussion:

1. What is a myth? What is a legend? Give an example of each. How do myths and legends differ from each other?

2. Be able to identify the gods and goddesses and places listed above and know what they are associated with. They will appear in later chapters of this book, but it will be helpful to you if you know something about them when you next meet them.

Introduction
The Gods of Greece
(continued)
Crossword Puzzle

Introduction
The Gods of Greece
(continued)

Across

1. messenger of the gods
4. goddess of Spring
8. split Zeus' head with his axe
10. goddess of love
12. rock
14. goddess of wisdom
18. where the gods lived (2 words)
19. ruler of the gods
20. watchdog who guarded the underworld
22. three sisters who made men gracious and wise
24. ruler of the seas
25. greatest of the Titans
26. Cronus was a _____
28. Artemis, Apollo's sister
29. Aphrodite's son (watch out for his arrows)

Down

1. wife of Zeus
2. the talking horse (we can't all be Greek gods...)
3. Poseidon ruled them another name for oceans
5. Poseidon carried one
6. ferryman across the Styx
7. god of the underworld
9. the bride of Hades
11. Titan who gave men fire
13. three sisters who punished the wicked
15. Titan who carried the world on his shoulders
16. Titan father of the sun and moon
17. three sisters who determined what happened to men
21. goddess of hearth and home
23. Diana's brother, god of the sun
27. god of war

Introduction
The Gods of Greece

(continued)

CAN YOU MATCH THESE?

Match the names of the following with the phrase that best describes them.

Aphrodite	the god of war
Eros	the messenger of the gods
Atlas	forged lightning for Zeus
Athena	chief of all the gods
Zeus	god of the underworld
Poseidon	god of the sea
Hades	goddess of the moon, and the hunt
Hephaestus	god of the sun and the light
Cerberus	goddess of love
Charon	goddess of wisdom
Persephone	Ferryman for the dead
Demeter	sisters who punished the wicked
Hera	Wife of Zeus
Hermes	Dog who guarded the underworld
Ares	Held the earth on his shoulders
Apollo	Beautiful wife of Hades
Diana	Son of Aphrodite, god of love
The Fates	sisters who determined what happened
The Graces	sisters who made mortals gracious
The Furies	Caused things to grow, helped by nymphs

Chapter I

DEUCALION AND THE FLOOD

Vocabulary:

nectar   oracle   forethought
ambrosia   lyre

People and Places:

He'be   The Muses   Pro-me'the-us
Deu-ca'li-on   Pyr'rha
Mount Par-nas'sus   Hel-lenes   Hel'las

For Discussion:

Much is often made of the fact that many ancient cultures had their own versions of a flood story. Have your student(s) compare the character of these false gods with that of the One True God. You might have them read the first chapters of Genesis. Have them compare the Greek stories of Creation and the Flood with the Biblical accounts. If your students are younger, you may need to read aloud to them, stopping to discuss as you go.

Older students might research the Creation and Flood stories from other cultures. Compare with the biblical account.

Chapter II

CADMUS AND THE DRAGON'S TEETH

Vocabulary:

capering   din
masons   realm
tufts

People and Places:

Phoe-nic'i-a   King A-ge'nor
Eu-ro'pa   Cad'mus
Thebes   Am'phi-on
Harmony

For Discussion:

1. How could you say that good came out of the disappearance of Europa? What part of the world bears her name today?

2. Tell the story of the founding of Thebes. Who founded it? How did it happen?

3. Cadmus was the founder of a very rich and prosperous city, yet he was not altogether happy. Tell why not. What was Cadmus' final end?

Chapter **III**

PERSEUS

Vocabulary:

quoits

People and Places:

Dan'ae	Per'se-us	Mediterranean Sea
Dic'tys	Pol'y-dec'tes	Gor'gons
Me-du'sa	The Grey Sisters	Hes-per'i-des
Se'ri-phos	An-drom'e-da	Cas'si-o-pe-i-a
Ar'gos	Ce'phe-us	

For Discussion:

1. Again we have a king who attempts to save his own life by exposing the innocent to almost certain death. Yet, when Perseus returns to Argos at the end of the story, he does not return in anger. Why not?

2. Why did Perseus go in search of Medusa? Why did Polydectes believe that Perseus would never return alive? How was Perseus able to succeed in his quest? Did Polydectes like his wedding present?

3. Describe the rescue of Andromeda. Who rescued her, what was she rescued from?

4. Find "the Great Bear," "Cepheus," "Perseus," and "Cassiopeia" on a star map.

Chapter IV

HERCULES AND HIS LABORS

Vocabulary:

girdle   errand   funeral pyre
kindled

People and Places:

Her'cu-les   Thebes   Eu-rys'the-sus
My-ce'nae   Au-ge'an Stables   Ar-ca'di-a
Am'a-zons   Hyp-pol'y-te   Atlas
The Fates   Al-ces'tis   De-i'a-ni'ra
Nes'sus

Background Information:

In the stories of Hercules, Jason, and Theseus there may be something of a transition between myth and legend and history. While Hercules seems to be a legendary character whose exploits remind us of the larger than life heroes of American tall tales. Theseus is, by tradition, considered to be the first ruler of Athens.

In Edith Hamilton's book, Mythology, she suggests that Hercules was the embodiment of the values of the majority of Greece outside of Athens. Theseus, she says, is the embodiment of things valued by the Athenians. In the study of these two figures, you might have your students compare the two, listing the values represented by each. Have them save the list and refer to it later when a more thorough study of Athens and Sparta is underway.

For Discussion:

1. How would you describe Hercules? What were his strengths of character? His weaknesses?

2. What would you expect a culture that glorified Hercules to be like?

Chapter **V**

JASON AND THE GOLDEN FLEECE

Vocabulary:

centaur   lynx   brazen (brazen-footed)
ointment   fleece

People and Places:

I-ol'cus   Black Sea
Jason   Ar'go-nauts
Pe'li-as   Or'phe-us
Phrix'us and Hel'le Cas'tor and Pol'lux
Hel'les-pont   Me-de'a
Col'chis   Si'rens

For Discussion:

1. An element recurring throughout Greek myths and legend is the king who fears that an offspring will one day cause him to lose something that he values (usually his life or his throne), and so decides to kill the child. Such attempts at infanticide are thwarted by a tender-hearted servant, and the child, raised in humble circumstances, returns to do the very thing the king had feared.
   You need to make your students aware that infanticide was practiced in Greece. Unwanted infants were usually left in remote places to die of exposure. Within the context of the story, you might want to discuss Pelias' motives for seeking Jason's death. (Notice how he died.)
   You might wish to draw (or lead your student(s) to draw) the obvious parallels between infanticide in Greece and the way in which unwanted infants are disposed of in our time.

(continued on next page)

Chapter V
JASON AND THE GOLDEN FLEECE
(continued)

2. Why did Jason attempt to get the Fleece?

   Who were the Argonauts and how did they get their name? Name some of Jason's more famous companions. What was special about them?

   Describe the obstacles Jason had to overcome in order to get the Fleece. How was each overcome?

   Discuss the role of the gods in Jason's successes. Do you think he could have been successful on his own?

   What type of person do you think Medea was? Why did she choose to help Jason? (You might read other accounts of Medea in Edith Hamilton's Mythology, and Robinson Jeffers translation of Euripides' Medea. Medea proves to be a valued, though easily offended ally, and a very deadly enemy. Further study of tales that concern her would lay a good groundwork for discussion of the importance of choosing your friends and associates wisely!)

3. Find the constellation "The Twins" on a star map. Find out when it is visible in your area.

Chapter **VI**

THESEUS

Supplemental Texts:

The Penguin Atlas of Ancient Greece, pages 24-25, "King Minos and Knossos"

Vocabulary:

guardian	trident	devoured
hoist	ward off	tribute
solemnity		

People and Places:

Ce'crops	Ae'geus	The'seus
Club-bearer	Si'nis	Pro-crus'tes
Minos	Lab'y-rinth	A'ri-ad'ne
Ae-ge'an Sea		

Background Information:

The story of Theseus and the Minotaur may have some basis in fact. In early Greece, the most highly developed society was found on the island of Crete. Knossos was the capital city. The culture was very wealthy. King Minos was noted for his wealth and the luxury of his court. Women of Crete were very active in public life. The Mother of the Earth was the most important goddess, and there is some evidence that human sacrifices were a part of her worship. The Cretian priests wore bull shaped masks in their ceremonies, and bull dancing (a dance in which dancers would leap up and grab the bull's horns then somersault over the bull's head) was both a game and a part of religious service. Elements of this can be seen in the story of the Labyrinth.

It is unclear how Crete fell. There is evidence of an invasion in which the city was burned. Mythology says that Theseus brought about the fall of Crete when he destroyed the Minotaur.

For Discussion:

1. How would you describe Theseus? What were his strengths of character? His weaknesses?

2. What would you expect a culture that valued Theseus to be like?

3. Compare and contrast the character traits embodied in Theseus with those embodied in Hercules.

Chapter VII

AGAMEMNON, KING OF MEN

The next two chapters (VII & VIII) tell the story of the Trojan War. Chapter IX tells something of the wanderings of Odysseus as he returned home after the war ended. They are a summary of the tales included in the **Iliad** (the story of the war itself) and the **Odyssey** (the story of Odysseus' voyage home). There are several very good adaptations of these two works available for children. I recommend that you have your student(s) read the book length adaptations as well. You might also consider reading Homer's original (the English translation will have to do for most of us) aloud to your charges. Stopping with the chapter summaries is like reading only the Cliff Notes — all plot summary and little of the adventure.

With our elementary-aged children, we used Alfred J. Church's retellings and were quite pleased. He does a good job of maintaining the high tone of the original. For many years, his versions were out of print. Recently, Greenleaf Press republished Church's **The Story of the Iliad**, edited and updated by Cyndy Shearer. Perhaps, by the time you read this study guide we will have been able to reprint the **The Story of the Odyssey** as well. Until then, we think the best children's version in print of The Odyssey is **The Children's Homer** by Padraic Colum. You may be able to find one or more of these at your local public library:

> ***The Iliad for Boys and Girls***, by Alfred J. Church
> ***The Odyssey for Boys and Girls***, by Alfred J. Church
> ***The Children's Homer***, by Padraic Colum
> ***The Story of Ulysses***, A Landmark Book
> ***The Story of Troy***, by Roger Lancelyn Green

Once you have chosen your text, divide it up into daily reading assignments on the "Reading Assignment Chart" (see sample on page 57). Whether you read the book aloud or assign it as independent reading will depend largely upon the reading level of your student. If the child has a difficult time warming up to the book, try reading a few chapters aloud — stopping the story deliberately at some agonizing spot (make them beg!).

As you read (or as they read), discuss the wisdom and folly of the actions of the various characters in the story. Note the differences between bravery and brash recklessness. Who shows mercy? Who wants only vengeance? Just about any virtue or vice can be illustrated by someone or something somewhere in the story. For instance, if you choose to read *The Story of Ulysses*, be sure to note the reasons Menelaus uses in his attempt to draw Ulysses into the war. Much fertile ground for discussion there (Be sure to include James 4:1-ff in that discussion). *(continued on next page)*

Chapter VII
AGAMEMNON, KING OF MEN
(continued)

Supplemental Texts:

The Penguin Atlas of Ancient Greece, pages 34-35, "The Trojan Wars"

Vocabulary:

perplexed   javelins

People and Places:

My-ce'nae   Ag-a-mem'non   Paris
Pri'am   Aegean Sea   Helen
Men-e-la'us   Iph-i-ge-ni'a   A-chil'les

For Discussion:

1. How did the goddess of discord disrupt the wedding of Peleus and Thetis? How did Paris get involved? How was the conflict resolved?

2. What prophecy was made about Paris and Troy?

3. What reward did Paris choose? Was this a particularly wise choice? How did his choice cause even further discord?

4. How did the conflict come to be something more than a matter between Paris and Menelaus? (A discussion of the wisdom or folly of entering into entangling alliances might be appropriate here.)

5. Discuss the sacrifice of Iphigenia. Depending on the maturity of your students, you might want to compare this story with the account of Abraham and his willingness to sacrifice Isaac. One possible point of contrast: the reason the demand was made and what that says about the character of God and the character of the Greek goddess, Diana.

Chapter VIII

ACHILLES BRAVEST OF THE GREEKS

Vocabulary:

wares   havoc   pestilence
forge   avenge

People and Places:

A-chil'les   Hec'tor   Pa-tro'clus
Pal-la'di-um   Di'o-me'des   Si'non
the Trojan Horse   An-drom'a-che

For Discussion:

1. Who were Achilles' parents? How did Achilles' mother try to protect him? What did she miss? Why was she so determined to keep him out of the war with Troy?

2. Why were the other Greek princes so determined to have Achilles fight with them? How did Odysseus trick Achilles into betraying his disguise?

3. What misfortunes did the tenth year of the war bring to the Greeks? What did Patroclus do in attempt to help rally the Greeks when Achilles refused to fight? How successful was he?

4. What did Achilles do when he heard about Patroclus' death? How did his mother attempt, once more, to keep Achilles safe? How did he eventually die?

5. What was so significant about the Palladium? What happened to it?

6. Tell the story of the Trojan Horse.

7. Research Project: Did the Trojan War really happen?
    Michael Woods, ***In Search of the Trojan War*** would be good for teacher preparation and ideas about possible resources.

Chapter **IX**

THE ADVENTURES OF ODYSSEUS

Vocabulary:

siege   lotus   lull
squall   keen   swineherd
suitors

People and Places:

Ulysses   Te-lem'a-chus   Cyclops
Eu-ryl'o-chus   Cir'ce   Scyl'la
Cha-ryb'dis   Sic'i-ly   Ca-lyp'so
Ith'a-ca   Pe-nel'o-pe   Ae'o-lus
Strait of Mes-si'na

For Discussion:

1. What did Odysseus do to avoid joining the Trojan War effort? Why did he want to remain at Ithaca? How was he thwarted?

2. Retell the stories of Odysseus' encounters with the following:
   the lotus-eaters
   the Cyclops
   Aeolus
   Cir'ce
   the Sirens
   Scylla and Charybdis

3. Meanwhile, back at the palace, what was happening? How had Penelope avoided naming another to replace Odysseus? When Odysseus discovered what was happening, what did he do? How did the way the suitors treated the "poor beggar" reveal their character?

4. Choose some scene or incident from Odysseus' journey home and write a play, a radio drama, or news story about it. Tape the radio drama. Either make a tape of the news story (read it aloud as if it were a news broadcast) or put it together with other stories and illustrations for the front page of a newspaper.

Chapter X

LYCURGUS

Background Information:

1. As the populations of various invading peoples (Ionians, Dorians, etc.) mingled and moved into Greece, Crete, Cyprus and the Aegean Islands, they settled into isolated villages. The chiefs of the tribes eventually ruled as kings, advised by village elders. The villages had no armies, as such. All citizens (that is, the men who were not slaves) were soldiers. The soldiers had the right to vote on matters regarding war and peace. The advisory role of the elders became increasingly important as time went on.

2. The scarcity of food was a continuing source of trouble. The land was rocky and mountainous. The nobles might own olive groves, but wheat was very scarce. Meat was eaten only on special occasions. Primarily, the diet consisted of porridge and fruit.

3. Citizen Assemblies had some limited strength. All free men belonged. As was said before, initially, they had the right to vote on whether or not to go to war. Eventually, they began to demand new laws, more land, more food, and lower taxes. Those kings who listened and gave in to the Assemblies' demands lasted significantly longer than those who did not.

4. By 500 B.C. most Greek cities had tried just about every type of government a person could be ruled by — democracy, oligarchy (rule by nobility), kingdoms, tyrants. When Theseus died, Athens organized into an oligarchy with a chief magistrate, known as an Archon. In time, the number of archons increased to nine. Rulers, however, were bound by no written laws.

5. By this time, most of the Greek cities were organized into what are called "city-states." The Greeks had very definite ideas about the importance of their individual "Polis," or city. Because of the ruggedness of the Greek landscape, the cities were generally isolated from each other. Those people who were not members of a city were considered its enemies. War and disputes between cities were constant.

(continued on next page)

Chapter X
LYCURGUS

Background Information:
(continued)

A person's worth was measured by his association with a polis. It was his home and the home of his gods. It was his work, protection, entertainment, and his only reason for living. It was in short his first priority. This attitude is also present in Roman culture. The great desirability of having Roman citizenship grows out of this attitude. (A reading of Philippians 3:20 and Hebrews 11:8-10 would be appropriate reading here. Note the differing attitudes toward earthly dwelling places.)

6. The two most famous/important Greek city-states were Athens and Sparta.

Supplemental Texts:

The Penguin Atlas of Ancient Greece, pages 48-49, "Rise of the City-States"

Vocabulary:

regency	propose	barley
oligarchy	feeble	temperance
flinch	effeminate	idlers

People and Places:

Pel'o-pon-ne'sus	Spar'ta	Ly-cur'gus
Helots		

For Discussion:

1. What was important to the Spartans? Cite specific examples. What was their attitude toward the weak or the deformed? Describe the education of Spartan children.

2. How did Lycurgus feel about wealth and luxury? What did he do in an attempt to discourage the Spartans from seeking after wealth?

4. For further reading on Sparta, see V.M. Hillyer's *A Child's History of the World*, "Hard as Nails," pages 79-83.

Chapter XI

DRACO AND SOLON

Background Information:

In 700 B.C., Athens was an unimportant, small city. Attica, the country around the old fortress was ruled by nobles who owned the villages and groves, quarrelled constantly, and treated the people like slaves. During those constant quarrels, they would frequently set fire to their own crops, burning up a years' supply of food in just one day. To make matters worse, there were no written laws on which a standard of justice could be based.

If a baron claimed the land that an endebted farmer owned, the case went to a council of judges made up of a committee of other barons. ("The dwarves are for the dwarves!" to quote C.S. Lewis.) If the sale of the land did not cover the debt, the man was sold into slavery.

Once Athens began to trade with money instead of bartering, nobles were more interested in selling food abroad. Thus, food became very scarce at home. Farmers were forced to borrow, went deeper and deeper into debt, and usually lost their land. People demanded laws that would protect them. In 621 B.C., the nobles chose Draco to write a code of laws for the city. The laws were not especially well received. If a man stole a fig from a baron's orchard, the penalty was death. Draco was asked if he thought it was fair to give a murderer and a thief the same punishment. He is said to have replied, "Death is the proper punishment for a thief. It is unfortunate that nature has not given us a harsher one for a greater criminal."

The laws written by Solon were met with great approval.

Supplemental Texts:

The Penguin Atlas of Ancient Greece, pages 58-59, "Athens Ascendant"

Vocabulary:

slight	mortgaged	archons
prosperous	yoke	

(continued on next page)

26

Chapter XI
DRACO AND SOLON
(continued)

People and Places:

Dra'co	So'lon	Assembly
Senate of Four Hundred Croe'sus		Lydia

For Discussion:

1. Have your student(s) compare and contrast the laws written by Draco with those written by Solon. For further comparison, you might read the Ten Commandments. What would your student(s) say is the most important things to include in written laws? You might have them write their own set.

2. Discuss Solon's definition of happiness. Do you agree or disagree with him?

Chapter **XII**

PISISTRATUS THE TYRANT

Supplemental Texts:

The Penguin Atlas of Ancient Greece, pages 56-57, "Rise of the Tyrants"

Vocabulary:

dissuade   citadel   tyrant
minstrels

People and Places:

Pi-sis'tra-tus   A-crop'o-lis

For Discussion:

1. In what ways did Pisistratus set out to make himself the "master of Athens?" What do you think of his actions?

2. How would you compare the three rulers of Athens you have just read about? Would you rather live under Solon, Pisistratus, or Draco? What were the strengths and weaknesses of each man?

3. During this same time period, the prophet Daniel is living in Babylon serving Darius the Mede, who ruled Babylon under Cyrus. Compare Daniel with Pisistratus.

Chapter XIII

MILTIADES
THE HERO OF MARATHON

Supplemental Texts:

The Penguin Atlas of Ancient Greece, pages 74-75, "Persian Campaigns I"

Vocabulary:

soverign	heralds	marathon	
avenge	expedition	obliged	seige

People and Places:

Hip'pi-as	Hip-par'chus	Da-ri'us	
Mar'a-thon	Aegean Sea	Mil-ti'a-des	Pa'ros

For Discussion:

1. What kind of rulers were Pisistratus' sons?

2. Tell how Darius came to be involved in the conflict between the people of Athens and Hippias. How was Darius' "help" received throughout Greece? How were his messenger's treated?

3. This Darius is also known as Darius Hy-stas'pes. It is the same Darius mentioned in Ezra 6:6-12. The rebuilding of the temple in Jerusalem was completed in the sixth year of his reign. According to Unger's Bible Dictionary, the Darius that Daniel served under was known as Darius the Mede who ruled Babylon under Cyrus.

4. The soldier who ran from the battle field to the city was named Pheidippides. In the modern Olympic games, the marathon is a race in which athletes run twenty-two miles without stopping, the same distance Pheidippides ran. It is named in honor of Pheidippides' famous run. Find out how far twenty-two miles is from your house. How would you like to run that far without stopping? You might also do a report on other famous marathon runners.

(continued on next page)

Chapter XIII
MILTIADES THE HERO OF MARATHON
(continued)

5. How was it that the little Greek army was able to defeat the Persians? Who was the commander of the Greeks? Though most Athenians were delighted by the news brought by Pheidippides, another group of folks were not. Why weren't they pleased, and what did they do when they heard the news? How were their plans thwarted?

6. To whom did the Athenians give credit for their victory over the Persians?

7. Tell what happened to Miltiades after the Persians went home.

Chapter **XIV**

LEONIDAS AT THERMOPYLAE

Supplemental Texts:

The Penguin Atlas of Ancient Greece, pages 76-77, "Persian Campaigns II"

Vocabulary:

gymnasium	strait	scourged
impassable	sulphur springs	vast
plundered		

People and Places:

Le-o-ni'das	Xer'xes	Sar'dis
Hel'les-pont	Ther-mop'y-lae	

For Discussion:

1. Why didn't Darius return to Greece after the battle at Marathon? Who came in his place, and who did he bring with him?

2. How did the Persians get across the Hellespont?

3. The Persians intended to march through the pass at Thermopylae. What stood in their way? Tell how they got through. (You might want to make a model of the pass and show how the soldiers were positioned in order to see how so few men could really hold off such a larger force. You could make it out of modeling clay. When you are through, reenact the battle — using your model, of course.

4. After Thermopylae, what happened to Athens?

5. Xerxes is known in the Bible as Ahasuerus, the husband of Esther. You might read the book of Esther together with your student(s) for more information about him.

Chapter XV

THEMISTOCLES

Vocabulary:

oracle   cleft   proposed

People and Places:

The-mis'to-cles   Mount Par-nas'sus   Pyth'i-a
Ce'crops   Sa'la-mis   At'ti-ca
Ar'gos

For Discussion:

1. In the last chapter you learned that Xerxes' men found Athens mostly deserted. Where was everybody?

2. Tell the story of how Themistocles came to build his "wooden walls."

3. Where did Themistocles want to meet Xerxes? How did Themistocles get him there? Why do you think Xerxes fell for the secret message?

4. On a large piece of construction paper, draw the strait of Salamis. Using two different colored or shaped objects (bean and pennies, or some such), reenact the battle of Salamis. Show how it was that the Persian fleet was defeated. Pretend you are Xerxes watching from your throne.
   How do you feel, O Great King?

5. Tell how it was that, later in life, Themistocles came to be a Persian ruler.

Chapter XVI

ARISTIDES THE JUST

Vocabulary:

rival	ostracism	ostrasize
banished	earthenware	ravaging
fortified	enormous	outlay

People and Places:

A-ris'ti-des	Thes'sa-ly	Pla-tae'a

For Discussion:

1. Describe the relationship between Aristides and Themistocles.

2. What is ostracism? How was it practiced in ancient Athens?

3. What were the "Liberty Games," and why were they held?

4. What was significant about finding that the olive tree had not been destroyed?

5. From what you have read, do you think Aristides deserved to be called "The Just?"

Chapter **XVII**

CIMON

Vocabulary:

theatrical exhibitions   expedition   disembarked
spoil (noun)   Helots   maimed
banished

People and Places:

Ci'mon   Asia Minor
Aes'chy-lus   Soph'o-cles

For Discussion:

1. How did Cimon show his support of Themistocles' "wooden walls?"

2. What did Cimon do to help Athens? How did Athens respond to him?

3. What were the "long walls?" What was their intended purpose?

4. Tell how Cimon came to be banished.

5. You are a writer for the Athenian Daily Press. Your editor has just told you to write Cimon's obituary. What could you write to best summarize Cimon's character and actions?
    Do you think Athenians treated him fairly? Decide how your opinion will affect your article.

Chapter XVIII

PERICLES

Supplemental Texts:

The Penguin Atlas of Ancient Greece, pages 94-95, "Perikles and the Athenian Empire"

Vocabulary:

rival	jury	provisions
fortifications	desolated	

People and Places:

Per'i-cles	Cor-cy'ra/Cor-fu'	Cor'inth
Pe-lo-pon-ne'si-an War	Isthmus of Corinth	Phid'i-as
He-rod'o-tus	Thu-cyd'i-des	

For Discussion:

1. What was the relationship between Cimon and Pericles?

2. List some of Pericles' accomplishments.

3. Which of Pericles' activities upset the Spartans? What did this displeasure lead to?

4. How did the "Long Walls" serve Athens during the Peloponnesian War?

5. Which of his accomplishments gave Pericles the most satisfaction as he looked back over his life?

6. Who was Phidias, and what is he remembered for?

7. What is the "Golden Age of Pericles?" Why was it called that, and how long did it last?

Chapter XIX

ALCIBIADES

Supplemental Texts:

The Penguin Atlas of Ancient Greece, pages 98-99, "Peloponnesian War - Sicily"

Vocabulary:

Olympiad	herald	assemblage
lisp	fop	frivolous
bust	venture	lieutenant
Olympic Games	Peloponnesian War	

People and Places:

Al-ci-bi'a-des	Hel-les	Syr'a-cuse
Ni-ci'as	La-ma'chus	Persia
Asia Minor	E'lis	

For Discussion:

1. Tell about the history of the Olympic games — who did the Greeks believe established them? When and where did they first take place? How often were they held? Who could compete? How important did the Greeks think the games were?

2. Alcibiades was something of a celebrity. How did he become so admired? How would you describe his character? Give examples from his life that would support your description of him.

Chapter **XX**

LYSANDER

Vocabulary:

admiral   cunning   blockaded
desolate   refuge   defied

People and Places:

Ly-san'der   Ko'non   Ae-gos' Po-to'mos (Goat's River)
Pi-rae'us   Thu-cyd'i-des   The Thirty Tyrants
Thra-sy-bu'lus   Thebes

For Discussion:

1. Discuss the meaning and possible applications of Lysander's proverb: "When the lion's skin is too short, you must patch it with that of a fox."

2. Tell how the strategy Lysander used against Athens fit his proverb.

3. Discuss Sparta's treatment of conquered Athens. Why would the Spartans choose to tear down the Long Walls on the anniversary of the Battle of Salamis?

4. Would you like to live under the rule of the Thirty Tyrants? Explain your answer.

5. What do the cities of Thebes and Argos have to be proud of?

6. How did Lysander die? What did his death prevent?

Chapter **XXI**

SOCRATES

Note: After reading this chapter, try introducing your students to Plato's account of Socrates' life and death. Recommended Dialogues:

"Euthyphro" — (Dover edition, p. 1; Penguin edition p. 7) Socrates discusses the true meaning of piety, attempting to answer the question, "What is good?" This dialogue gives a feel for Socratic dialogues and humor (i.e. how to make mincemeat out of your opponent with style and grace). It's fun. This dialogue also illustrates the Socratic method of teaching in which the teacher asks the students questions with the intention of leading the student to discover the truth of a matter for himself, inductively.

"The Death of Socrates" — this is contained in the dialogue titled "Phaedo" (Dover edition, p. 55; Penguin edition p. 109). Socrates explains why he will not attempt to escape and why he does not fear death. He discusses his reasons for believing that the soul is immortal.
This is a very moving piece, but rather long (60+ pages). You will want to summarize much of this for younger students, but make sure you read the last twelve pages (Dover edition, p. 113; Penguin edition p. 173) which describe Socrates' farewell to his friends and his death.

Before you begin to read either of these aloud to your students, you should read them through yourself and see what passages you could skim and summarize for them. Some spots move slower than others.

As you read aloud, stop fairly frequently and ask questions such as:

What did he just say? What was his answer?
Why did he say that? What did he mean by that?
Was that a wise or foolish response? Why?

Have students paraphrase a short section so that no one gets lost. If you feel that you are getting bogged down in the middle of a section, summarize it and skip through so that you are able to keep moving.

(continued on next page)

Chapter XXI SOCRATES

(continued)

Don't underestimate your child's (or your own!) ability to follow this. It will be well worth your effort. Although Socrates and Plato were not writing out of a biblical mindset, you can still (and should) frame your discussion of the dialogues in the context of biblical truth. As to an appropriate age level for such a study — we worked through the two recommended dialogues with our third grader and some wonderful discussions grew out of the reading.

Supplemental Texts:

The Trial and Death of Socrates by Plato

Vocabulary:

philosophy   hemlock

People and Places:

Soc'ra-tes   At'ti-ca   Thrace
Xan'thip-pe   Ar-i-stoph'a-nes De-los'
Pla'to

For Discussion:

1. What did Socrates teach? How did Socrates differ from other Athenians? From other teachers in Athens? Why did some Athenians hate him?

2. What was Socrates charged with doing?

3. Socrates is often pointed to as a pagan philosopher who, however imperfectly, rejected the worship of many gods. He taught and argued that there could logically be only one true God. Lead your students in a discussion of this. Apply his discussion of piety in "Euthyphro" to what your students know about the nature of Greek deities.

Chapter **XXII**

XENOPHON

Vocabulary:

plight   sentries

People and Places:

Art-a-xer'xes   Cy'rus   Sar'dis
Bab'y-lon   Black Sea

For Discussion:

1. How would you describe Xenophon?

2. Pretend that you are a Greek soldier. Tell the story of the march to Babylon and back as a Greek soldier might have told it through his journal entries.

Chapter **XXIII**

EPAMINONDAS AND PELOPIDAS

Supplemental Texts:

The Penguin Atlas of Ancient Greece, pages 100-101, "Sparta and Thebes"

Vocabulary:

chief (as in "chief pleasure")   citadel
garrison   consequence   exiles

People and Places:

Pe-lop'i-das   E-pam-i-non'das   Cad'me-a
Ar-ca'di-ans   Thes'sa-ly
Man-ti-ne'a

For Discussion:

1. Describe the friendship of Pelopidas and Epaminondas. Can you think of other such friendships in history?

2. What was the relationship between Sparta and Thebes? How did it change?

3. What do you notice about the way Sparta behaves toward the people she conquers? What does that say about the character of her people? Do you think she behaves wisely? Defend your answer.

4. Who helped Sparta? How? What was their fate?

Chapter **XXIV**

PHILIP OF MACEDONIA

Note: It would be very much worth your while to obtain a copy of John Gunther's children's biography of Alexander the Great from the Landmark series by Random House. It includes a great deal of detail about the character of Philip (and Olympias and Alexander). Reading it can lay the foundation for some very valuable discussions on how Alexander's unwillingness to exercise self control eventually undid him.

The "Landmark Book" is entitled ***Alexander the Great***. Most public libraries have this one.

Supplemental Texts:

The Penguin Atlas of Ancient Greece, pages 106-107,
"Philip and Macedonian Expansion"

Vocabulary:

garlands	twined	phalanx
hedge	bristled	aroused
eloquence	orator	

People and Places:

Ma-ce-don'i-a	Philip	O-lym'pi-as
De-mos'the-nes		

For Discussion:

1. How would you describe Philip?

2. Draw a diagram or make a model of a phalanx. (You don't need to include all 1,000 men unless you really want to.) What was the significance of the phalanx?

3. Who was Philip's chief opponent? How did he oppose Philip?

4. How did Philip die? (NOTE: It is generally agreed that the assassin was hired by his lovely wife, Olympias.)

Chapter XXV

ALEXANDER THE GREAT

Supplemental Texts:

The Penguin Atlas of Ancient Greece, pages 120-121, "Campaigns of Alexander;" pages
122-123, "Alexander the General"

Vocabulary:

soothsayers	overawed	subdue
submission	expedition	procession
Levites	commercial	brazen
obliged	barren	signet ring

People and Places:

Bu-ceph-a-lus	Hel'les-pont	Gor'di-us
Dar'i-us	Is'sus	Tyre
Jerusalem	Alexandria	Babylon
Su'sa	India	Khai'ber Pass
Por'us	Rox-an'a	Bac'tri-a

For Discussion:

1. The story of Alexander and Bucephalus is one that is often told. What does this story illustrate about Alexander's character?

2. What was thought to be the significance of the burning of the temple of Diana at Ephesus?

3. Tell about Alexander's conquest of Greece.

4. Describe Alexander's treatment of Darius. What does Alexander's behavior toward Darius and his family show about Alexander? How did Alexander usually treat those he conquered?

5. When it is said, "Alexander had conquered the East, but the East had also conquered Alexander," what is meant?

6. On a map, show the route Alexander followed to the River Hydaspas. Shade in the territory conquered by him. Why did he not go any further? How long did it take Alexander to do all that he did?

Chapter XXVI

DEMOSTHENES

Vocabulary:

delicate
passages (of poetry)
rouse
magistrates
rhetoric

oration
orator
Philippic
pardon

stammered
gestures
propose
quill

People and Places:

Demosthenes   Thucydides

For Discussion:

1. Tell how Demosthenes trained himself to speak well. Is there anything in his methods that you could apply to your own study?

2. What was Demosthenes' criticism of Philip and Alexander? Give any examples you can. What was his advice to Athens concerning them?

3. How did Demosthenes react to the news of Philip's death?

4. How did Alexander respond to Demosthenes — his first strategy and his second strategy? How successful was Alexander against Demosthenes?

5. Describe the events that led up to Demosthenes' death? Tell how he died.

Chapter **XXVII**

ARISTOTLE, ZENO, DIOGENES AND APELLES

Vocabulary:

tutor   stoic   epicure
cynic

People and Places:

Ar'i-sto-tle   Sto'ics   Ze'no
Di-og'en-es   A-pel'les
Per'ga-mos

For Discussion:

1. Name one famous man who studied under Aristotle.

2. Why did Aristotle flee Athens?

3. Tell what happened to Aristotle's writings.

4. Contrast the Stoics with the Epicurians.

5. What did the cynics teach? Who was their teacher?
   Describe Diogenes.

Chapter XXVIII

PTOLEMY

Supplemental Texts:

The Penguin Atlas of Ancient Greece, pages 128-129, "New Kingdoms, New Rivalries"

Vocabulary:

sovereigns	accustomed	pith
commerce	astronomers	circumference
diameter	fascinating	
celebrated (as in a celebrated person)		

People and Places:

Pto'le-my	Pto'le-my Phil-a-del'phus
Cle-o-pat'ra	

For Discussion:

1. Who was Ptolemy? Where did he rule? Name three things we remember him for doing.

2. Name two important things done by Ptolemy Philadelphus.

3. On a map, mark the location of Ptolemy's canal.

4. Why did Alexandria become known as an important center of learning? What is the length of the earth's circumference? What is the diameter of the earth? Why would that be useful information?

Chapter **XXIX**

PYRRHUS

Vocabulary:

truce   engines

People and Place:

Pyr'rhus   Ep-i'rus
A-dri-at'ic Sea   Ar'gos
Arch-i-me'des   Si'ci-ly

For Discussion:

1. What was Pyrrhus' goal for his life? Why do you think he would set this goal? Is this a goal you would want to set for your life? Do you think that such is a wise goal to set? Explain your answer.

2. What did Pyrrhus mean when he said, "Another such victory and I shall have to go home?" Tell how the war ended.

3. Tell how Pyrrhus died. Did he reach his goal?

4. Research the life and accomplishments of Archimedes. Make a report of your findings. Draw or make a model of his stone-throwing engine. Be able to explain how it worked.

Chapter XXX

CLEOMENES III

Vocabulary:

ephors   usury   persuade

People and Places:

Cle-om'en-es III   A-gi-a'tis   King A'gis
Leonidas   Lycurgus   A-chae'an League

For Discussion:

1. Describe Cleomenes wedding. Why did he doubt that his wife would ever love him? Did his worst fear come to pass?

2. What changes did Cleomenes make in Spartan life? How did the Spartans feel about these changes? What do you think about them?
   What were the advantages/disadvantages and would you like to live under such a set up? Explain your answer.

3. How did Cleomenes rule come to an end? What became of him and of Sparta?

Chapter XXXI

THE FALL OF GREECE

Supplemental Texts:

The Penguin Atlas of Ancient Greece, pages 132-133, "Roman Conquest"

Vocabulary:

province   logic

For Discussion:

1. What kept Greece from overcoming the Macedonians? Was this a new or recurring problem for the Greeks? Explain your answer and give examples that support it.

2. How did Macedonia fall? What did Athens, Thebes, and Sparta become?

3. After Rome fell, who ruled Greece? When did Greece become an independent nation again?

4. What would you say is the greatest accomplishment of the Ancient Greeks, that is, the most valuable contribution they have made to the world?

5. Who would you name as the best of all the men you have read about it in this book? The worst? Explain your answer.

Student _____   Date _____

READING ASSIGNMENT CHART

Topic_____

Book Titles:

    (1)_____

    (2)_____

    (3)_____

Date	Book/Chapter	Pages

Copy as many of these as you need as you plan your study.

CHRONOLOGICAL OVERVIEW
of Greek History

B.C.

3000-1400	MINOAN CULTURE DOMINATES
	Center was island of Crete.
	    2500-2200 — Old Kingdom in Egypt;
	    2130-1800 — Middle Kingdom in Egypt;
	    1575-1100 — New Kingdom in Egypt)

1160-1150	MYCENAEAN CULTURE
1200	FALL OF TROY

1200-1900	Barbarian invasions. Dorian invasion.
	Greek settlement of Aegean islands and west coast of Asia Minor.
	    Israelites first settle in Canaan
	    1000-960 King David;
	    960-931 King Solomon

900-700?	COMPOSITION OF HOMERIC POEMS sometime during this period
859-650	KINGS REPLACED BY OLIGARCHIES
776	Beginning of list of victors in Olympic games.
750-550	Colonization 744-612 — Assyrian Empire at its height.
700	Hesiod Sparta in control of all southern Peloponnese.
650-500	OLIGARCHIES OVERTHROWN BY TYRANTS Sargon, King of Assyria conquers Cicilia and Syria. (Fall of Israel
593	SOLON'S REFORMS IN ATHENS
560-510	PISITRATID TYRANNY IN ATHENS Belshazzar's party interrupted by an uninvited hand. Daniel interprets.
547	Persian conquest of Lydia.

CHRONOLOGICAL OVERVIEW of Greek History

(continued)

BC

500-325	Attic red-figure pottery. CLISTENES RULES ATHENS, introduces ostracism
500	Revolt of Ionian cities from Persians.
492-497	UNDER DARIUS, THE PERSIANS ATTEMPT TO CONQUER GREECE. BATTLES: 　MARATHON, 490 　THERMOPYLAE (Under Xerxes, Darius' son) 　SALAMIS, Himera, 480 　Plataea and Mycale, 479 RULERS: 　Athens — Themistocles and Aristides 　Sparta — Leonidas
478	Organization of Delian League Smaller states paid money to Athens for the support of her navy — beginning of Athenian empire.
461-430	PERICLES IN POWER. 　Sophocles (playwright) 　Euripides (playwright) 　Herodotus (historian) 　The Sophists (philosophers) 　Phidias (sculptor)
431-404	PELOPONNESIAN WAR 　Aristophanes (bawdy comic playwright) 　Socrates (philosopher) 　Hippocrates (of Hippocratic Oath fame)
404-371	Spartan preeminence in Greece. Chief wars, 400-386 and 379-371
399	EXECUTION OF SOCRATES.
393	Rebuilding of the Long Walls of Athens.
371-362	Theban preeminence. PLATO

CHRONOLOGICAL OVERVIEW of Greek History

(continued)

BC

359-336	REIGN OF PHILIP II OF MACEDON. DEMOSTHENES ARISTOTLE
357-355	Revolt of Athens' eastern Aegean allies, instigated by Mausolus of Caria.
338	PHILIP OF MACEDON IN CONTROL OF GREECE.
336-323	REIGN OF ALEXANDER THE GREAT.

323-276	WARS FOR CONTROL OF PARTS OF ALEXANDER'S EMPIRE.
	Emergence of Ptolemaic, Seleucid, and Antigonid Kingdoms under Alexander's three top generals.
	Last flowering of Athenian culture:
	    portrait statues, Tanagra terracottas, new comedy
	    Epicurus (philosopher)
	    Zeno (philosopher)

279-278	Galatians overrun Macedonia, northern Greece, and Thrace, then cross into Asia Minor.
274-241	Syrian Wars I-III.
270	ROME IN CONTROL OF ALL GREEK CITIES IN ITALY.
241	End of Rome's first war with Carthage. Rome acquires most of Sicily.
241-221	Decay of Egypt. Defeat of Macedonia. Dynastic wars in Seleucid Kingdoms.

A Few Words About Greenleaf Press

Greenleaf Press was founded by Rob & Cyndy Shearer in 1989. It was born of their frustration in searching for a history program for their children that was at the same time challenging, interesting, and historically accurate. They were looking for a curriculum that would begin at the beginning and present history in a logical, readable, chronological way. None of the available programs satisfied them. They discovered that the best history books for children they could find were, sadly, out of print. The best of the out-of-print classics were really terrific. They told interesting stories about real people. And the Shearers discovered that their children loved history when it was presented in the form of an interesting story about a real person.

And so, they founded Greenleaf Press — to bring back to life some of the wonderful biographies which had been used to teach history so successfully in the past. ***Famous Men of Greece*** and ***Famous Men of Rome*** were Greenleaf's first publications. Those two books have now been joined by ***Famous Men of the Middle Ages***, ***Famous Men of the Renaissance and Reformation*** (written by Rob), and ***Famous Men of the 16th & 17th Century*** (also by Rob).

Shortly after reprinting ***Famous Men of Rome***, faced with questions from many people who liked the *Famous Men* books, but wanted help in HOW to use them, they decided to publish Study Guides showing how to integrate biographies, activities, and reference material. There are *Greenleaf Guides* available for the Old Testament, Egypt, Greece, Rome, the Middle Ages, and the Renaissance and Reformation, all written by Rob & Cyndy Shearer.

From that day to this, Greenleaf Press has remained committed to "twaddle-free", living books. We believe that history is both important and exciting and that our kids can share that excitement. We believe that if our children are to understand the roots of our modern-day, mixed-up world, they must study history. We're also thoroughly convinced that studying history with our children provides us with a wonderful opportunity to reflect with them on moral choices and Godly character.

Scope & Sequence

Seven Year Plan

1st Grade - Old Testament (Historical Books: Genesis – Kings)
2nd Grade - Egypt (& Old Testament Review)
3rd Grade - Greece and Rome
4th Grade - The Middle Ages and The Renaissance
5th Grade - The Reformation and The Seventeenth Century (to 1715)
6th Grade - 1715 to 1850
7th Grade - 1850 to The Present

Six Year Plan

2nd Grade - Old Testament and Egypt
3rd Grade - Greece and Rome
4th Grade - The Middle Ages and The Renaissance
5th Grade - The Reformation to 1715
6th Grade - 1715 to 1850
7th Grade - 1850 to The Present

Five Year Plan

3rd Grade - Old Testament, Egypt, Greece & Rome
4th Grade - The Middle Ages and The Renaissance
5th Grade - The Reformation and The Seventeenth Century (to 1715)
6th Grade - 1715 to 1850
7th Grade - 1850 to The Present

Four Year Plan

4th Grade - Old Testament, Egypt, Greece & Rome
5th Grade - The Middle Ages, The Renaissance, and The Reformation
6th Grade - 1600 to 1850
7th Grade - 1850 to The Present

Teaching History with Living Books
An overview of our
Study Guides and History Packages

The Greenleaf Guide to Old Testament History

The history of Israel ought to be the first history studied by every child. This Guide outlines a daily reading program that using all of the historical books of the Old Testament. The focus is on history — not theology. The historical books of the Bible always focus on a central character. History in the Old Testament is built around a series of biographies and character studies. The Old Testament really could be subtitled "Famous Men of Israel." Thus, the Study Guide discussion questions focus on "What actions of this person are worthy of imitation?" "What actions should we avoid?" "What is God's judgment on this life?"

There are 180 readings, one for each day of the school year. The readings are designed to give the student (and parent/teacher) an overview of the history of Israel and an introduction to the key figures whose lives God uses to teach us about Himself and His character. These stories are intended for children in the elementary grades, and should be accessible, even to children in kindergarten or first grade (though they make a rich study for older children, even teens and adults)! If this seems surprising, the reader is reminded that God's plan for families is for fathers to teach these stories to their children. When God decrees in Deuteronomy 6:6-7 that "you shall teach them diligently to your sons and shall talk of them when you sit in your house and when you walk by the way and when you lie down and when you rise up," He is not referring to math facts and grammar rules. God's textbook for children are the stories from the Old Testament. He is specifically referring to the story of the Exodus from Egypt, but by implication He means the entire Old Testament. The Old Testament is God's textbook for children. This is the only textbook, quite probably, Jesus used during his education in the house of his parents.

Duration: One full academic year

The Greenleaf Guide to Ancient Egypt

Ever wonder how Biblical history and Ancient Egypt fit together? Why was God so angry with Pharaoh anyway? This makes a perfect second history unit for students. Or, as an alternative, you could pause in your study of Old Testament history and study Egypt after you have finished the story of Joseph in the book of Genesis. This unit has ten lessons, including one devoted to the rediscovery of Egypt and the development of the science of archaeology in the 19th century. There is also a lesson on the Exodus in the context of Egyptian culture. The main text for the study is the Landmark book, ***The Pharaohs of Ancient Egypt***, which includes biographies of the following Pharaohs:

Cheops (builder of the Great Pyramid)
Hatshepsut (His Majesty, Herself!)
Thutmose III (the Napoleon of the
   Ancient World)

Aknaton (the monotheistic Pharaoh)
Tutankamon (the boy-Pharaoh)
Rameses II (Smiter of the Asiatics)
Duration: approximately 15 weeks

Famous Men of Greece

If you were to have asked a citizen of ancient Greece to tell you something about the history of his nation, he would have begun by telling you about his gods and the myths and legends told about them. Even though the events described in the myths did not actually happen in the way the story says, the Greek myths will tell you much about what was important to the people who told them.

Greek culture forms the backdrop to all the events of the New Testament. Paul was educated not just in the teachings of the Rabbis, but also in the writings of the Greeks. He was able to quote from literature in his speech to the men of Athens. Many of the details in his letters become richer and more significant when understood in the context of Greek culture.

Famous Men of Greece covers the following chapters:

Introduction: the Gods of Greece
Deucalion and the Flood
Cadmus and the Dragon's Teeth
Perseus
Hercules and His Labors
Jason and the Golden Fleece
Theseus
Agamemnon, King of Men
Achilles, Bravest of Greeks
The Adventures of Odysseus

Lycurgus
Draco and Solon
Pisistratus the Tyrant
Miltiades the Hero of Marathon
Leonidas at Thermopylae
Themistocles
Aristides the Just
Cimon
Pericles
Alcibiades
Lysander

Socrates
Xenophon
Epaminondas and Pelopidas
Philip of Macedonia
Alexander the Great
Demosthenes
Aristotle, Zeno, Diogenes, Apelles
Ptolemy
Pyrrhus
Cleomenes III
Duration: approximately 15 weeks

Famous Men of Rome

Rome was the political super-power of the ancient world. Rome history spans 500 years as a kingdom, 500 years as a Republic, and 500 years as an Empire (when Rome was ruled by military dictators who called themselves "Caesar"). It was the Pax Romana of the Empire that allowed the Gospel to spread rapidly to every corner of the earth. And it was the example of the Roman Republic which inspired the United States' Founding Fathers.

Famous Men of Rome covers the following individuals:

Romulus
Numa Pompilius
The Horatii and the Curiatii
The Tarquins
Junius Brutus
Horatius
Mucius the Left-Handed
Coriolanus
The Fabii
Cincinnatus

Camillus
Manlius
Manlius Torquatus
Appius Claudius Caecus
Regulus
Scipio Africanus
Cato the Censor
The Gracchi
Marius
Sulla
Pompey the Great

Julius Caesar
Cicero
Augustus
Nero
Titus
Trajan
Marcus Aurelius
Diocletian
Constantine the Great
End of the Western Empire
Duration: approximately 15 weeks

Famous Men of the Middle Ages

When the power of Rome was broken, the tribes of barbarians who lived north of the Danube and the Rhine took possession of the lands that had been part of the Roman Empire. These tribes were the Goths, Vandals, Huns, Franks and Anglo-Saxons. From the mixture of Roman provinces, Germanic tribes, and Christian bishops came the time known as The Middle Ages and the founding of the European nation-states.

Famous Men of the Middle Ages covers the following individuals:

The Gods of the Teutons
Alaric the Visigoth
Augustine of Hippo*
Attila the Hun
Genseric the Vandal
Patrick of Ireland*
Theodoric the Ostrogoth
Clovis
Justinian the Great
Two Monks: Benedict
  and Gregory
Mohammed
Charles Martel
Charlemagne
Harun-al-Rashid

Egbert the Saxon
Rollo the Viking
Alfred the Great
Henry the Fowler
Canute the Great
El Cid
Edward the Confessor
William the Conqueror
Gregory VII & Henry IV
Peter the Hermit
Frederick Barbarossa
Henry the Second and
  His Sons
Louis the Ninth
St. Francis and St. Dominic

Robert Bruce
Marco Polo
Edward the Black Prince
William Tell
Arnold Von Winkelried
Tamerlane
Henry V
Joan of Arc
Gutenberg
Warwick the Kingmaker
Duration: approximately 15 weeks (though many families supplement this study with literature readings and extend it to a full year).

Famous Men of the Renaissance and Reformation

The Middle Ages were not the "Dark Ages." Yet there had been substantial changes in Europe from 500 to 1300 AD. Rome and her Empire fell. The Germanic tribes moved into the old Roman provinces and established feudal kingdoms. Many of the Roman cities declined in population or were abandoned. Gradually, much of the literature and learning of the classical world was lost and forgotten. Around 1300, in the towns of northern Italy especially, a group of men began to devote themselves to the recovery and revival of the classical world.

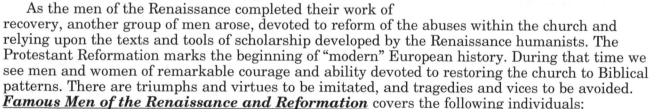

As the men of the Renaissance completed their work of recovery, another group of men arose, devoted to reform of the abuses within the church and relying upon the texts and tools of scholarship developed by the Renaissance humanists. The Protestant Reformation marks the beginning of "modern" European history. During that time we see men and women of remarkable courage and ability devoted to restoring the church to Biblical patterns. There are triumphs and virtues to be imitated, and tragedies and vices to be avoided.

Famous Men of the Renaissance and Reformation covers the following individuals:

Renaissance
Petrarch
Giotto
Filippo Brunelleschi and
  Donatello
Lorenzo Valla
Cosimo D' Medici
Lorenzo D' Medici
Girolamo Savonarola
Sandro Botticelli
Leonardo Da Vinci
Cesare Borgia

Niccolo Machiavelli
Leo X (Giovanni De Medici)
Albrecht Durer
Michelangelo Buonarroti
Erasmus
Reformation
John Wyclif
Jan Hus
Martin Luther
Charles V
Ulrich Zwingli
Thomas Muntzer

Conrad Grebel & Michael
  Sattler
Melchior Hoffman, Jan
  Matthys & Menno Simons
Henry VIII
Thomas More
William Tyndale
Thomas Cromwell & Thomas
  Cranmer
John Calvin
John Knox
Duration: Approximately 15 weeks

Graphical Timeline of Ancient History

by Robert G. Shearer
© 1996 Greenleaf Press

Key Dates

Israel

c.1900 B.C. –	Joseph sold into slavery
c.1445 B.C. –	The Exodus
c.1000 B.C. –	Death of Saul, David becomes King
605-536 B.C. –	The Exile

Egypt

2500 B.C. –	Khufu (Cheops) The Great Pyramid
1505-1484 B.C. –	Queen Hatshepsut
1361-1344 B.C. –	Amenhotep IV also known as Akhenaton
51-31 B.C. –	Cleopatra

Greece

c.1200 B.C. –	Siege of Troy
478-404 B.C. –	Civil War between Athens & Sparta
356-323 B.C. –	Alexander

Rome

753 B.C. –	Founding of Rome
509 B.C. –	Founding of the Roman Republic
100-44 B.C. –	Julius Caesar
312-327 A.D. –	Constantine
410 A.D. –	Sack of Rome by the Visigoths
476 A.D. –	Death of the last Roman Emperor

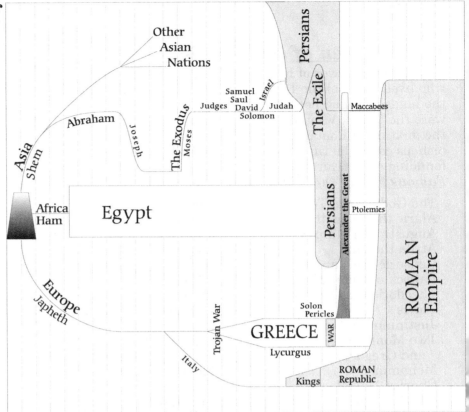

Graphical Timeline of Medieval History

Key Dates

England:

c.400 –	Romans withdraw
793 –	Sack of Lindisfarne by Vikings
871-899 –	Alfred the Great
1066 –	Norman Conquest
1339-1453 –	Hundred Years War
1455-1485 –	War of the Roses

France:

482-511 –	Clovis
714-41 –	Charles Martel
768-814 –	Charlemagne
1180-1223 –	Philip II Augustus
1412-1431 –	Joan of Arc

Germany:

936-937 –	Otto I, the Great
1152-90 –	Frederick I Barbarossa
1210-50 –	Frederick II, Stupor Mundi
1493-1519 –	Maximilian
1516-1556 –	Charles V

Italy:

440-461 –	Pope Leo I
480-543 –	St. Benedict
590-640 –	Pope Gregory
1073-85 –	Pope Gregory
1200-1240 –	St. Francis
1309-1378 –	Babylonian Captivity (of the Papacy)
1378-1417 –	The Great Schism
1096 –	1st Crusade
1147 –	2nd Crusade
1189 –	3rd Crusade

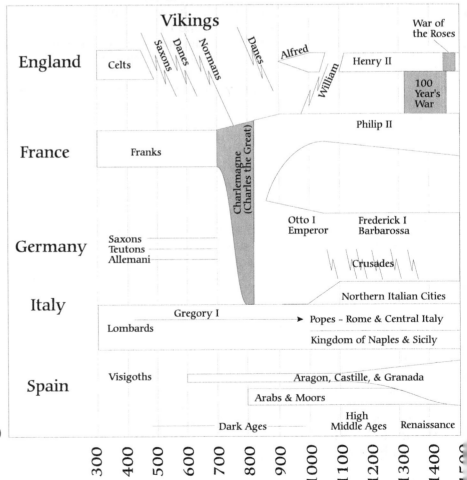

Made in the USA
Las Vegas, NV
16 March 2025

19654819R00037